LANDSCAPES ON A TRAIN

Cole Swensen

LANDSCAPES ON A TRAIN

NIGHTBOAT BOOKS
NEW YORK

ISBN: 978-1-937658-41-0

All images: Cole Swensen

Design and typesetting by Margaret Tedesco
Text set in Gotham and Bitstream Cooper

Cataloging-in-publication data is available
from the Library of Congress

Distributed by University Press of New England
One Court Street
Lebanon, NH 03766
www.upne.com

Nightboat Books
New York
www.nightboat.org

Landscapes on a Train

Green. Cut. And I count: the green of the lake the green of the sky and the field

Which is green and is breaking. Waking out of an opening, a sudden field opens

Out with a suddenness that instantly places us miles away across a field of wheat.

Light. All accident. All pours down. Across a rolling green, soft in animals. Soft
In water, which is also green. Some small grey that arcs away, way back before
Roads. Poplars in rows. Poplars in double rows lining roads no longer there.
And farther trees in silhouette rowing off the top of a ridge.

The light is an accident because the trees are old. So without wind with grain.

Orchard grain on light. Orchard lined the heart. A spire, a forest, a village made

By hand. And another stand of trees, of hay in rolls in fields. In every distance is

Sieved and moves off slowly, a long thin line that trains the eye. A line of hills that

Pulls away.

Shore as it pulls away. There's a grey lake below the grey sky. Hundreds of grey

Trees lining the banks of a stream. Stream down sun in little coins. A bigger town.

A church too big for its hill. And cows easing down the slope. Slows its calm, and

More little sun goes on among selves.

A window opens a train. Now on whiter air. Other measures drift. Quick, hasp

And fast the green comes back, innumerably strong. Swung the sky off light. Light

The one comes down. To a single ray in a single field. Divides and buries on. A

Train across open land opens night. (A train lands all night across an open field.)

The reflection on the window across is almost as sharp in the dark and the light

Runs aground. Caves in in little chips. Like birds. Birds smalled down to words

Come back. Flowered in cloud. Out like somewhere on that lives.

Trains pass behind a screen of trees, trees blind and leaving trees. Nothing is so

White as what is seen in the dark against a darkness that replaces space and wavers

In pieces, a landscape almost held. Small by the landed tree. By things that move

More slowly than trees.

Renders night through rain. Ricochets. Away from the dark and from the perfect. Light

Leaves the perfect. There in the dark. Animals move smoothly along their chosen paths.

A road disappears, a curve that, in curving, carves. Cows along. A graze it comes

Close if this precise and loud the birds besides, cried alive, are off, they are from

Now on, twenty blind spots in the black trees alight.

Trees with leaves green backed by silver. Turning wherever the light, what small

Light, is taken in. Tree with light painted on. Then tree with points of dark which

Are birds or fruit that build slowly up into a night.

There once was a church. There once was a steeple. These things fall into landscape.

And then there were none. Canal across one. One white bird. Go on. And so it goes.

A church in the middle of a field is a tree. Poplar poplar. Hundreds of swans. White

Is a tiny gash. All over the swan is light striking an arc. Or any animal that adamant.

Emphatic crows in a field. Three. And then dozens are the dark. Are the traveling

Folded. Intricate folding apart.

Horse beside a river. Standing perpendicular. And crossing the river next, a wind.

Next, a field. Guessed against the grain. You could have painted it. You are painting

A long line of horses until they're gone.

And orchard on. Trees count. One more house. Fallen down. Goes falling on. One
More canal the size of a thumb. And the singular way that trees take over a meadow.
All that walking. All it calls. I heard something call. One if animal. And horses once
More a plain cut by a rivulet. A house stands alone in a field.

A white cow stands alone in a field. A white horse stands alone among trees. A

Line of trees stands alone. In sheaves of green. As the eye strikes a far thing, a

Small thing, a thing at this distance becomes distance alive all alone.

So white is just a wall. This is just before dark and the stone bridge. And what is

That white thing out there in the field? Fielding light. Wall of chalk. Chalk wall

With all the stones taken out. Along a stone road. Swept up a hill streaked with

Green.

Planes of migrating geese. The geese are hundreds, they are sheets, hundreds of

Feet up there are two sheets of geese only barely each other and shifting screens,

The infinite splitting of finite things.

Light keeps up. Light touch on building, light builds on. On the inside of the window.

Cut and form. Most colors amount to this without names. It happens in sun and there

Is little else.

Pale bond. Grain runs. Embarks upon. It's mostly rain and we pass on. Past a

Tossing road through a stand of hay. Stand among graves. Stand trees in a line

Migrating through rain, the rain first a green and then a form.

A lake folds. And so holds sky. At which a tower stood and now stands older than

Higher, through which it rises. All around its ruined farm.

Cows turn to crows in a field alone. Dovecote grey in wind, now mill, now wall

In the hedgerows a birdhouse. All the hares are facing east. And the cows walking

Left between. Five men building a stone wall. Stones the size of hands. And shape.

The hands and the stones are equal parts of the wall.

Slip of line in roads through trees. Cut into lives. In the rupture of an aqueduct

The light yet. Moves. Chateau-grey. With the aviary buttered on, ruptured in,

Caught abroad in a slip that brings. The sky back down to the ground.

Hay breaking a field broken red. And there goes a village of sand. Broke

The ruined ruin. Cored the left hoof round, left sound, left the green alive

With houses, small, all stone and backing up on a green built of dust.

White flock over the field just set. In a scattering flood. Over the field just

Horses on all sides and two white horses walk the silence in half. Against

A sky oddly sifted, and later pass. Down a lane that curves and then comes

Across.

And against, a sail now cuts. Open its own reflection. Each pane opened, sliced,

And then shines. Its shine timed. And through it flew the sun. Through it, herd

And run, the hills. The boats are going blue.

Moreover the black crows strike. Is over and the trees go even. Even farther

Down the burning field, all three. White birds against the trees. Evening results

In a motion of sorts, a sort of splintering air. Lights from a train that passes its

Little windows through a sieve. Little houses in the sky. Flowers on a bridge all

White. All white birds. All white moves.

Light slices across the tops of trees. White light cuts the presence back. The lack

Thereof. Light replaced. Light that is an approach. That we can't see the light enter

The cells of the trees, nor what leads, the path down to the cells below the trees.

One green is the only living grey. Sun down harsh, one small town, one farm

Down to a single standing house in the sun, standing warm. A tree of two hands.

More windmills where the sky breaks down. A small white car and no sound.

Seven horses. Is not the same nor the same number are seven horses turned

To trees. Makes a forest you can see through a forest light in things. Bends

Down the sun down on a river swimming with horses all taken for wind.

Effect of noon: even the edges; the edges are even, even precise. All water is

Necessarily precise. Mistletoe crowding the emptiness of the empty branches

Of emptied trees. Slicing evenly the thin light shredding the ribbons of thin

Light to strings.

Six or seven buildings and their six or seven bare trees. Beneath a large white

House in a hurl of green. In its pillars at a distance, clicking up stillness, the roof

Of sky that makes the sky turn slate into suddenly birds, solid birds holding on

To the sky.

The long broad river winds off, turns back on itself, copper muscle, lead mirror

That much earlier. Making the water walk over the meadow like a line of bare

Poplars walks over a field. Where a man who walks faster than the trees in the

Grey mist into which the trees recede.

Quiet lights the fog, washes the grey. Grey, the green that could have been rain.

A long line of greenhouses and small boats tied up to the bank, young plants under

Canvas arches another river passes, fewer boats and a house built for summer will

Rain upon rain.

River aground. Flat green boats among pollarded trees. More greenhouses marking

Color or missing a pane of the missing greenhouse, tarnished silver in the missing

Sun. These are not windows alone.

Old stone building on a hill is its weight, is still upheld, then taller and then stone

Blind until left lined up in pieces beside a standing bird, a lamp in another, and

Another, and then each shattered part lighting the length of the river causing dark.

White gates standing open to the river to the bridge in brick and stone and matching

White boat. The boat takes part, creates an equation between bridge and gate, an

Equivalence sealed by a white horse running toward a white house, its front door

Open in the rain.

The sun is a thrush, thrust up against, is falling in sheets, it falls in and sees

Three rows of trees slipping past like passing screens, the screens slip on vast

Thin walls of rain. Of doors. You slide the screens to change the world.

Which yet retains its lines and remains migrating trees through a heap of rain.

White arches cross a river. Weigh it down. River of trees that turns

Its back on. A collection of crows to the touch. Season extant, season

Alarmed. The surface of water: a matter of light. Bright. Wash across

Buildings facing the face across. A face is crossed by light.

That distance will live all the trees into rooms. All the room in trees grates

The winter to edges. One tree in winter combs all winter to pieces, very fine

Pieces that fall from sky to sky, sharpening the sky.

The unfurled sight of empty paths. Empty slight in its rising, a road of grey slicing

Haze and the other river low, all the way across clouds crossing below, a line

Making the sky a straight line running along a fold.

Birds toward the sea, a sea of them. Which is a private thing. A man sings as he

Walks along. A field away. His breath stands out, the black of a bird alone. The

Bird is as black as the only one.

The migratory route of the seed: Small farm painted thereon. White. Small

Orchard held in flock. Held in strain in lines it counts, gaining force of trees

Walked off, and to what the trees belong. When you looked up the trees had gone.

Leaves or is seen receding. Black car down a black road. More piles of more stone,

Nest. Boats in neat rows. Row through the early morning on a loss of form.

Miniature horses in three corrals. Heads down. A field in flower, the yellow

Just a little, shredding through. And a tower or something that was once a

Tower harvested into birds over time. Now all the horses back into birds that

Climb. They climb past the line of lights evenly spaced. The line of lights stays.

Almost black at five p.m. A track. Of trees as darker masses of the river in fact.

Onto falling light. Barely a difference. Turning another darkness in places torn.

From light keeping time. Light is a device to keep time in line.

The lights of a landing plane the streams of lights lining a road of a town the lights

Of a single light of a farm. Everything cannot be light, a light, we pass through

Miles of dark.

Rain draws. In colors halved all color dies. Down. To a sound, which has no shore.

So far gives in in grains. Rain rains down upon rain.

The sun goes back to glass. The roil of birds alive inside. The sky in flying light. Huge

Piles of leaves in the live sky burning the piles of flames into light dying in the sun.

Sun slicing. Hangs the wind in shapes. It saw a horse drink and a taller horse

Next. A dozen horses in an open field, open horse and on into the hand-made time

Of a horse lying down in a field.

Across the small canal the gated sun without sound the water poured itself from land.

Walking dark. All living things in the dark line up. They march. That tracks the

Rain. The spherical that. The man across from me slightly shakes. He thinks

It's his hands. He shakes, and then he shakes them.

Once a swan is lost on a road. The lost road curves and runs aground. And so on.

A map on the wall that forms the end of the train, and so, on it goes. A series

Of birdhouses tall on their poles.

Flowering cherry, and the trees with white flowers are pears. The entire abandoned Farm. Plum. At the bottom of five gardens in a row. Rowing up the river, a man, in Time, turns to space. By any means necessary.

Little inlet, little grounded cloud. Of white, off-white, off-cloud, standing at rest

And poise. And large, a white bird, aquatic, loud. Along an inlet headed inward.

With the silence of a window.

Seagulls land on their feet. This is a world of things. Three egrets. One much

Taller than the other two. Three trees erode the sky. Raw, strong roads that

Sweep the wind.

Blue heron in slow motion over half an ocean the ocean is slow and it rises blue

Against grey water, but water is nothing in the sky but the birds one often alters

Their reflections carved across the surface of the sea.

New stone. A fence almost glints. Under trees a stone house underneath a magnolia

Could not be less than five of them for at least a day or so as they flower from bone.

A graveyard in the sun is always time. And in time the new stone slows down

And the white gains. Pieces in the grey. In flower are the birds. Caught small

As they take off each one, one inch across. And the tree stops. The birds are rain

And the grey tree is a white stain.

ACKNOWLEDGEMENTS

Warm thanks to the editors of the following journals for your support
of this work—at times in earlier versions:

The American Reader
Asymptote
Black Warrior Review
Conjunctions
Critical Quarterly
Iowa Review
Koshkonong
Lana Turner
The Laurel Review
Plume
Vacarme
The Volta

And to Jeremy Sigler, for the invitation to participate in the catalogue:
Figuring Color, Institute of Contemporary Art, Boston, Spring 2012.

Warm thanks as well to Donna Stonecipher and to Shari DeGraw
for their advice and help at various stages.

Cole Swensen is the author of 13 books of poetry, including *Gravesend*, and a book of essays, *Noise That Stays Noise*. She's also the co-editor of the 2009 Norton anthology *American Hybrid* and the founder and editor of La Presse, a nano-press dedicated to contemporary French work in translation. She is professor of Literary Arts at Brown University.

NIGHTBOAT BOOKS

Nightboat Books, a nonprofit organization, seeks to develop audiences for writers whose work resists convention and transcends boundaries. We publish books rich with poignancy, intelligence, and risk. Please visit our website, www.nightboat.org, to learn about our titles and how you can support our future publications.

The following individuals have supported the publication of this book. We thank them for their generosity and commitment to the mission of Nightboat Books:

Elizabeth Motika
Benjamin Taylor

In addition, this book has been made possible, in part, by grants from The Fund for Poetry, The National Endowment for the Arts, and The New York State Council on the Arts Literature Program.

State of the Arts
NYSCA

ART WORKS.

National Endowment for the Arts
arts.gov